S0-AVG-915

Nelson Mandela

Terry Barber

ACTIVIST
SERIES

Text copyright © 2006 Terry Barber

Photographs copyright © in the names of individual photographers, artists, and organizations as noted specifically on page 48.

All rights reserved. No part of this book may be reproduced or transmitted in any form or by any means, including photocopy, recording, or any information storage and retrieval system, without the prior written permission of the publisher.

Nelson Mandela is published by
Grass Roots Press, a division of Literacy Services of Canada Ltd.

PHONE 1–888–303–3213
WEBSITE www.literacyservices.com

ACKNOWLEDGEMENTS

We acknowledge the financial support of the Government of Canada through the Book Publishing Industry Development Program (BPIDP) for our publishing activities.

We acknowledge the support of the Alberta Foundation for the Arts for our publishing programs.

Editor: Dr. Pat Campbell
Image Research: Dr. Pat Campbell
Book design: Lara Minja, Lime Design Inc.

Library and Archives Canada Cataloguing in Publication

Barber, Terry, date
    Nelson Mandela / Terry Barber.

(Activist series)
ISBN 1–894593–49–9

    1. Readers for new literates. 2. Mandela, Nelson, 1918–.
3. Presidents—South Africa—Biography. I. Title. II. Series.

PE1126.N43B362 2006   428.6'2   C2006–902897–4

Printed in Canada

Contents

Nelson looks out his cell window.

Nelson Mandela

His life is hard. The prison food
is bad. His 7-by-7-foot cell is cold.
He must work hard. His health
gets worse. His spirit suffers. But he
never gives up. His spirit will not die.
His name is Nelson Mandela.

Africa

SOUTH AFRICA

Nelson Mandela is born in South Africa.

Early Life

Nelson Mandela is born on July 18, 1918. He is born in South Africa. White people rule South Africa. Black people have few rights. As Nelson grows up, blacks lose even more of their rights.

Nelson's African name is Rolihlahla. This name means "trouble-maker."

Two people plow a field.

Early Life

Nelson grows up in a small village.
He looks after cattle and sheep.
Nelson plows fields. After his chores,
he plays soccer. He learns to fish.
Nelson is never hungry. He has a
good life.

Nelson's village is called Qunu.

An elder tells a story.

Early Life

Nelson's father is a chief. Nelson's father talks with the elders. Nelson listens to their stories. They tell stories of life before the white people came. They tell stories of how the white people stole their land. These stories teach Nelson about the past.

These homes do not have running water.

City of Gold

Nelson moves to Egoli in 1941. Egoli means "City of Gold." Nelson lives in a small room. It has a dirt floor. It has no running water. Most black people live this way. In the City of Gold, there is no gold for black people.

Egoli is also called Johannesberg.

Mandela works in his law office.

City of Gold

Nelson works in a law office. He is a clerk. Nelson wants to be a lawyer. In 1947, Nelson becomes a full-time student. He gets his law degree in 1952. He opens a law firm.

Nelson opens the first law firm for black people.

The ANC hold a meeting.

City of Gold

Nelson also enters politics. He wants to help his people. Nelson joins the ANC. The ANC wants to change South Africa. The ANC wants blacks to have equal rights. This group gives black people hope.

The ANC stands for African National Congress. Black people form the ANC in 1912.

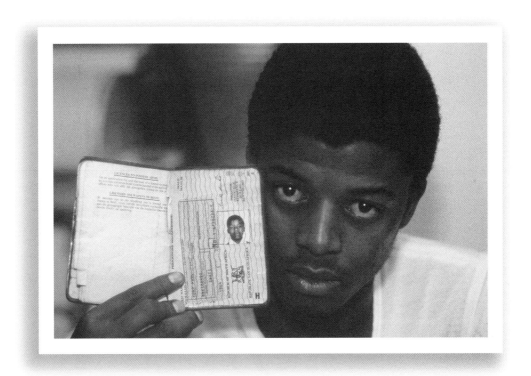

This man shows his pass book.

Apartheid

Most of the people in South Africa are black. Yet, white people rule the country. In 1948, the National Party comes into power. Life becomes worse for black people. The government makes **apartheid** laws. These laws are not fair to black people.

The white rulers give pass books to black people. These books say where black people can live and work.

The black and white people cannot sit together.

Apartheid

Apartheid laws keep black and white people apart. They cannot marry each other. They cannot go to the same school. They cannot even sit together.

The apartheid laws are **racist.**

The government bans black leaders.

Freedom Fighter

Nelson speaks against apartheid.
He is a great speaker. Black people
listen to him. Some white people do
too. Some whites agree with Nelson.
The ruling whites do not.

The government **bans** Nelson in 1953. He cannot go to meetings. He is told he cannot speak to groups.

Nelson gives a speech.

Freedom Fighter

Nelson wants a better life for black people. He thinks speeches will bring change. He thinks marches will bring change. He thinks strikes will bring change. He thinks **boycotts** will bring change. Nelson is wrong.

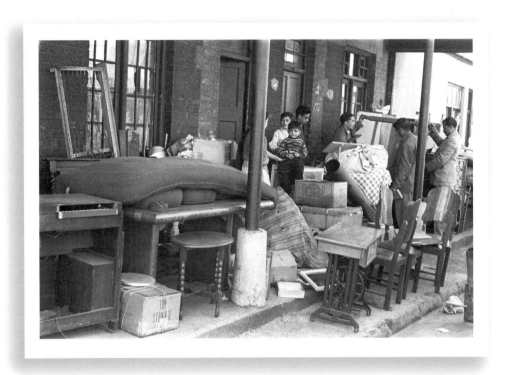

In 1955, the police order these people to leave Sophiatown.

Freedom Fighter

More than 60,000 people live in Sophiatown. This town is near Egoli. The police order them to leave Sophiatown.

The black people do not want to leave their homes. Nelson plans **protests.** The protests do not work. The police make the black people move.

Nelson's army bombs this power line.

Freedom Fighter

Nelson decides to "fight fire with fire." He forms an army in 1961. The army destroys property. It bombs railroads and power plants. The army does not want to take lives. It wants white people to listen. The army wants equal rights.

The army is called the Spear of the Nation.

This is Nelson just before he goes into hiding.

Freedom Fighter

The violence does not bring change.
The ruling whites want to stop
Nelson. They want to put him in jail.
Nelson goes into hiding in 1961.
Nelson moves from safe place to
safe place. He cannot live with his
wife and children.

Nelson
hides for
17 months.

Nelson walks to the treason trial.

Freedom Fighter

The police hunt for Nelson. They find
Nelson in 1962. The police arrest him.
Nelson is found guilty of **treason.**
He gets life in prison. He gets a life
sentence for his beliefs. He gets a life
sentence for wanting equal rights.

Nelson talks to an inmate at prison.

Nelson Goes to Prison

Nelson goes to a prison on Robben Island. He works out each morning. He studies at night. He teaches other **inmates.** The inmates also learn from each other. The prison becomes known as "Mandela University."

Nelson goes to prison at age 46.

These men use a pickaxe to break stone.

Nelson Goes to Prison

Nelson works hard in prison. He breaks stone with a pickaxe. As he gets older, his back hurts. He gets sick. His blood pressure is high. Nelson loses 50 pounds. He suffers for years.

The police try to break up this riot.

Nelson Goes to Prison

The black people in South Africa also suffer. They want apartheid to end. Black people riot. South Africa is coming apart. Whites are afraid they will lose their way of life. White rulers know that apartheid cannot go on.

These people want the white rulers to free Nelson.

Nelson Goes to Prison

In prison, Nelson's fame grows. People feel it is not right to keep Nelson behind bars. People around the world want South Africa to free Nelson. The white rulers know they must free Nelson.

This rock is in a park in the U.S. The rock says "Free Nelson Mandela."

Nelson and his wife Winnie walk together
after he leaves prison.

Nelson is Freed

It is February 11, 1990. Nelson is
71 years old. He is freed from prison.
He has been in jail for 27 years.

Nelson, the president of South Africa, gives a speech.

Nelson votes
in the 1994 election.

Nelson is Freed

The people in South Africa vote for a new leader. In 1994, Nelson becomes the first black president of South Africa. Nelson has made life better for black people in South Africa. He is one of the world's greatest leaders.

In 1994, black people in South Africa vote for the first time.

45

Glossary

apartheid: a system of racist laws in South Africa.

ban: an official order that forbids something.

boycott: refusal to use a service or buy a product.

protest: to complain about something.

racist: a belief that one race is superior to others.

treason: to betray one's country.

Talking About the Book

What did you learn about Nelson Mandela?

What did you learn about apartheid?

What does freedom mean to you?

Would you risk your life for your freedom?

Nelson Mandela decides to "fight fire with fire." What do you think this means? Do you think it was a good decision?

How did Nelson Mandela make the world a better place?

Picture Credits

Front cover photos (**center photo**): David Turnley/CORBIS; (**small photo**): © UWC-Robben Island Mayibuye Archives. **Contents page** (**top right**): © UWC-Robben Island Mayibuye Archives; (**bottom left**): © Courtesy African National Congress; (**bottom right**): © James P. Blair/National Geographic Image Collection. **Page 4:** © David Turnley/CORBIS. **Page 8:** © Lori Waselchuk/South Photographs /africanpictures.net. **Page 10:** © James P. Blair/National Geographic Image Collection. **Page 12:** © UN/DPI Photo. **Page 14:** © Jurgen Schadeberg/Drum Social Histories – Baileys African History Archive/africanpictures.net. **Page 16:** © BAHA/Drum Social Histories – Baileys African History Archive/ africanpictures.net. **Page 18:** © UN/DPI Photo. **Page 20:** © UN/DPI Photo. **Page 22:** © Drum Social Histories – Baileys African History Archive/ africanpictures.net. **Page 24:** © Drum Social Histories – Baileys African History Archive/africanpictures.net. **Page 26:** © Bob Gosani/Drum Social Histories – Baileys African History Archive/africanpictures.net. **Page 28:** © BAHA/Drum Social Histories – Baileys African History Archive/africanpictures.net. **Page 30:** © AP. **Page 32:** © BAHA/Drum Social Histories – Baileys African History Archive/ africanpictures.net. **Page 34:** © Drum Social Histories – Baileys African History Archive/africanpictures.net. **Page 36:** © Benny Gool – Oryx Media Productions/ africanpictures.net. **Page 38:** © Bienjamien Karlie/africanpictures.net. **Page 40:** © Paul Weinberg – South Photographs/africanpictures.net. **Page 42:** © Greg English/AP. **Page 44** (**top photo**): © UN/DPI Photo; (**bottom**): © Courtesy African National Congress. **Page 45:** UN/DPI Photo.